COMBATING TERRORISM: THE LEGALITY, UTILITY AND MORALITY OF COERCION

by

Colonel David Astin
United States Army

Dr. Larry Goodson
Project Adviser

This SRP is submitted in partial fulfillment of the requirements of the Master of Strategic Studies Degree. The U.S. Army War College is accredited by the Commission on Higher Education of the Middle States Association of Colleges and Schools, 3624 Market Street, Philadelphia, PA 19104, (215) 662-5606. The Commission on Higher Education is an institutional accrediting agency recognized by the U.S. Secretary of Education and the Council for Higher Education Accreditation.

U.S. Army War College
CARLISLE BARRACKS, PENNSYLVANIA 17013

ABSTRACT

AUTHOR: Colonel David Astin

TITLE: Combating Terrorism: The Legality, Utility and Morality of Coercion

FORMAT: Strategy Research Project

DATE: 22 March 2012   WORD COUNT: 8,703   PAGES: 42

KEY TERMS: Torture, Enhanced Interrogation Techniques, Detentions

CLASSIFICATION: Unclassified

In the aftermath of the terrorist attacks on America on September 11, 2001, U.S. leaders were determined to avoid another strike against the nation. As part of their efforts in the ensuing Global War on Terror, America's leaders authorized the use of coercive techniques during prisoner interrogations to gain intelligence deemed crucial to national security. The policies and procedures that emerged have brought the legitimacy of coercive techniques, which some view as torture, to the forefront of the political debate. This paper focuses on the legality, utility and morality of coercive interrogation techniques employed for the sake of state security.

COMBATING TERRORISM: THE LEGALITY, UTILITY AND MORALITY OF
COERCION

Prior to September 11, 2001, a seemingly comprehensive network of

international treaties and domestic laws prohibiting torture were in effect, and the three

branches of the United States government had each played a key role in their

development. The military, an extension of the executive branch, embraced opposition

to torture as well by incorporating procedures into applicable regulations and field

manuals for handling prisoners in accordance with the framework of the Geneva

Conventions. Congress and the military itself had "placed out of bounds all coercive

interrogation" through adherence to Geneva, and the "executive branch, in pre-9/11

conflicts, largely put this understanding into practice."[1] As the leader of the free world

following World War II, America held the moral high ground in having shaped and built

the foundation governing torture over a period of decades. However, that foundation

would be altered dramatically following the events of September 11, 2001.

When Osama bin Laden's al-Qaeda terrorist network struck America on 9/11, the

country now faced a "new kind of enemy in the first war of the twenty-first century."[2] To

combat that enemy the Bush administration, according to former Vice President Dick

Cheney, "developed a program to gain intelligence from detained terrorists that saved

lives and prevented future attacks."[3] This program involved the use of coercive

interrogation techniques by the Central Intelligence Agency (CIA); in the opinion of

advocates such as Cheney, the "program was safe, legal, and effective."[4] To its critics,

the techniques constituted torture and were both immoral and ineffective. As stated by

President Barack Obama, "Brutal methods of interrogation are inconsistent with our values, undermine the rule of law, and are not effective means of obtaining information."[5]

This paper focuses on the legality, utility and morality of coercive interrogation techniques employed for the sake of state security. In exploring the manner in which America abandoned its pre-9/11 position on coercive interrogation techniques, it reveals how the United States ceded the moral high ground that it had held and employed for decades as a key strategic strength.

The Legality of Coercion: 9/11 and Beyond

In the months immediately following the horrific 9/11 terrorist attacks on American soil, the administration of President George W. Bush was greatly concerned about the possibility of future strikes against the United States. As Bush stated, "the immediate task … was to harden our nation's defense against a second attack."[6] Frustrated by the perceived lack of intelligence it had obtained on al-Qaeda, the terrorist network that had perpetrated the 9/11 attacks, the administration began to consider a more aggressive approach to interrogation. A key element in interrogating members of al-Qaeda was a determination of their status in accordance with the Geneva Conventions. On January 18, 2002, White House Counsel Alberto Gonzales advised President Bush that the Department of Justice had issued a formal legal opinion on the matter. The opinion concluded "Geneva Convention III on the Treatment of Prisoners of War (GPWIII) did not apply to the conflict with al-Qaeda," and there were reasonable grounds to conclude GPWIII did not apply to the Taliban either.[7] There were dissenting views, most notably from Secretary of State Colin Powell. Powell believed the Geneva Conventions did apply and, furthermore, contended a conclusion to the contrary would encourage other countries to look for technical loopholes in future conflicts to determine they were not bound by Geneva either. After considering arguments for and against prisoner of war status, Gonzales determined that the "arguments for reconsideration and reversal are unpersuasive."[8] On February 7, 2002, Bush announced that he had accepted the legal conclusion of the Department of Justice and determined "Common Article 3 of Geneva does not apply to either al-Qaeda or Taliban detainees...."[9]

Bush's determination was based on advice from the Office of Legal Counsel (OLC). By delegation from the Attorney General, the Assistant Attorney General in charge of the Office of Legal Counsel provides authoritative legal advice to "the President and all the Executive Branch agencies. The Office drafts legal opinions of the Attorney General and also provides its own written opinions and oral advice in response to requests from the Counsel to the President."[10] Jack Goldsmith, head of the OLC from October 2003 until his resignation in July 2004, noted the "OLC is, and views itself as, the frontline institution responsible for ensuring that the executive branch charged with executing the law is itself bound by law."[11]

Goldsmith's predecessor at OLC was Jay Bybee who, along with OLC deputy chief John Yoo, wrote the January 2002 legal opinions that underpinned the president's decision regarding al-Qaeda and Taliban detainees. These would not be the last of Bybee and Yoo's questionable opinions. On August 1, 2002, they presented Gonzales with a memorandum regarding the standards of conduct under the United Nations Convention Against Torture, which the United States had signed in 1988.[12] That same day, they provided a classified memorandum for John Rizzo, acting general counsel of the CIA, regarding the proposed conduct of interrogations of Abu Zubaydah, the first "high-value" detainee since 9/11. Abu Zubaydah was an independent terrorist facilitator who helped run Khaldan, one of the many military training camps in Afghanistan tied to al-Qaeda. Given Abu Zubaydah's role as an important cog in the al-Qaeda network, the CIA made the decision to fly him to another country for interrogation at a secure location.[13] At issue was whether proposed CIA procedures for interrogating him would violate the federal statue prohibiting torture, specifically Section 2340A of Title 18 of the U.S. Code.

As legal scholar David Cole noted, there were reasonable aspects to the August 2002 memos. They were premised on the "unobjectionable claim that torture, both as a criminal and international law matter, is limited to a subset of all cruel, inhuman, and degrading treatment,"[14] a distinction also noted by the Convention Against Torture. Similarly, the memos maintained that in order for conduct to qualify as torture under the federal statute making torture a crime, it must be intended to inflict "severe physical pain or suffering" or "prolonged mental harm."[15] Cole further noted that those terms do not have objective benchmarks for when pain becomes severe or how long mental harm must last to be considered prolonged. However, in focusing on these critical statutory terms, OLC chose to use a federal health benefits statute for guidance, determining that "physical pain amounting to torture must be equivalent in intensity to the pain accompanying serious physical injury, such as organ failure, impairment of bodily function, or even death."[16] The OLC then applied this analysis to the Rizzo memo to approve particular interrogation techniques, to include waterboarding, requested by the CIA for gaining information from Abu Zubaydah.

Thus with the backing of the OLC decisions regarding the Convention Against Torture and the U.S. Code, CIA counterterrorism contractors waterboarded Abu

Zubaydah. This distinction made him the first person in American history known to have been waterboarded with the approval of a branch of the American government, specifically the executive branch and U.S. President George Bush.[17]

When Jack Goldsmith became head of OLC slightly more than one year after the memos had been written and approved, he reviewed them and found their conclusions to be deeply flawed and filled with numerous problems. Among the problems he identified was Bybee and Yoo's clumsy derivation of torture and "severe pain" from a health benefits statute unrelated to torture provisions. However, the opinion's major problem was that it went much further in stating, "Any effort by Congress to regulate the interrogation of battlefield detainees would violate the Constitution's sole vesting of the Commander-in-Chief authority in the President."[18] In Goldsmith's determination, this "extreme conclusion" had no foundation in any previous judicial decisions or any other source of law. Furthermore, it implied many other federal laws limiting interrogation and torture, to include the 1996 War Crimes Act and the Uniform Code of Military Justice, were essentially unconstitutional.[19]

As noted by Cole, the OLC memos chose the interpretations most likely to preclude any chance of criminal responsibility for CIA interrogators, regardless of how strained the interpretation, and it was "this consistent pattern of result-oriented reasoning … that is ultimately the most compelling evidence of bad-faith lawyering."[20] Goldsmith made a similar conclusion, stating the message of the August 1, 2002, OLC opinion was that "violent acts aren't necessarily torture; if you do torture, you probably have a defense; and even if you don't have a defense, the torture law doesn't apply if you act under color of presidential authority."[21] CIA interrogators and the agency itself, under pressure from the White House to get information about another attack, now had the "golden shield" of an OLC opinion.

In June 2004, Goldsmith withdrew the August 1, 2002, memo to Alberto Gonzales (the classified memo to Rizzo remained intact) as well as a subsequent memo in March 2003 containing much of the same analysis as its predecessor. He did so because, in his determination, "on an issue that demanded the greatest of care, OLC's analysis of the law of torture in the August 1, 2002, opinion and the March 2003 opinion was legally flawed...."[22] In spite of this, the Bush administration's program of what would come to be called "Enhanced Interrogation Techniques (EIT)"[23] had already begun in earnest, using the flawed opinions of Jay Bybee and John Yoo as legal cover.

The basis for the program of interrogation, as expressed in OLC's Rizzo memo, was to be the U.S. military's Survival Evasion Resistance and Escape (SERE) training. As noted by the U.S. Senate Committee on Armed Services in its inquiry into detainee treatment, during the resistance phase of SERE training, U.S. military personnel are "exposed to physical and psychological pressures ... designed to simulate conditions to which they might be subject if taken prisoner by enemies that did not abide by the Geneva Conventions."[24] The Senate inquiry cited a SERE instructor who acknowledged the training was designed in part on Chinese Communist techniques used against American prisoners during the Korean War to elicit confessions, most of which were false. The techniques to which SERE students are subjected include being stripped, being placed in stress positions, having hoods put over their heads, having their sleep disrupted, being subjected to loud music and flashing lights, and being exposed to extreme temperatures. It can also include face and body slaps and, until recently, waterboarding.[25] The report by the Senate made a critical distinction, which is that SERE techniques were not developed as a means of obtaining reliable information, but rather to better prepare U.S. military personnel to resist harsh interrogations.[26]

Administration officials failed to make this distinction; in spite of objections from several senior military lawyers, on December 2, 2002, Secretary of Defense Donald Rumsfeld signed authorization to put the aggressive SERE techniques into effect for detainee interrogations at Guantanamo Bay Naval Base, Cuba.[27] However, between mid-December and mid-January 2003, Navy General Counsel Alberto Mora repeatedly expressed his concerns to Department of Defense (DoD) General Counsel Jim Haynes that the interrogation techniques authorized by Rumsfeld "could rise to the level of torture."[28] Mora's determined efforts to have them eliminated were successful to a certain degree; on January 15, 2003, Rumsfeld rescinded the authority of Guantanamo to use the aggressive techniques. However, rescinding the authorization did not guarantee its effects would vanish. As U.S. Army Major General George Fay noted in his investigation into detainee abuse at Abu Ghraib, the Army doctrine for conducting interrogation operations was found in Army Field Manual 34-52, *Intelligence Interrogation*, but "non-doctrinal" techniques were developed for use in Afghanistan and "GTMO as part of the Global War on Terrorism (GWOT). These techniques ... became confused at Abu Ghraib and were implemented without proper authorities or safeguards."[29] In short, the road to abuse of detainees had begun with practices authorized for and implemented at Guantanamo.

The establishment of Guantanamo as the holding ground for detainees warrants examination given its highly significant role in the Global War on Terror. When the

United States began military operations in Afghanistan in October 2001, the American military and allied forces captured numerous Taliban and al-Qaeda fighters and placed them in prisons – often makeshift – throughout Afghanistan, and even on naval ships in the Arabian Sea. It quickly became apparent that these facilities could not securely hold the growing numbers of detainees, particularly after an uprising at Qala Jangi fortress in northern Afghanistan resulted in the death of CIA agent Johnny Spann and others; the prisoners took over the facility for a week until they were finally subdued. Other facilities contended with sniper fire and breakout attempts. Given such concerns, Bush administration officials selected Guantanamo Bay Naval Base, Cuba, as a detention site for dangerous detainees. Guantanamo was across the globe from the conflict in Afghanistan and in an isolated, well-defended location. In addition, "because it was technically not a part of U.S. sovereign soil, it seemed like a good bet to minimize judicial scrutiny."[30]

Not only would Guantanamo be used to hold Taliban and al-Qaeda detainees, it would be the site used for trials by military commissions, as announced by President Bush on November 13, 2001. As explained by law professor Christopher Pyle, military commissions differ from civilian trials in that they lack a jury and other procedural protection, most notably that evidence obtained through coercion is admissible. Pyle also noted military commissions have been used traditionally as a wartime tool, but the creation of new courts is assigned to Congress by the U.S. Constitution.[31]

Thus with a location (i.e., Guantanamo), a program to conduct interrogations, and a court system, the Bush administration had in place key elements in its foundation for combating terrorism. The foundation, however, rested in large measure on questionable legal interpretations from OLC, interpretations which were to be challenged in cases appearing before the U.S. Supreme Court. In *Hamdi v. Rumsfeld* (2004), the court ruled the president could exercise his traditional military powers to detain Yaser Hamdi, an American citizen. However, the court determined the executive branch did not have the power to hold indefinitely a U.S. citizen as an enemy combatant without basic due process protections, to include the ability to challenge his or her detention before a judge or other "neutral decision-maker."[32] Furthermore, the court ruled in *Rasul v. Bush* (2004) that foreign nationals imprisoned without charge at the Guantanamo Bay interrogation camp were entitled to bring legal action challenging their captivity in U.S. federal civilian courts.[33]

In spite of these decisions, the Supreme Court did not require the president to alter many of his actions. However, the court did send a signal to the president that "a state of war is not a blank check" for him in conducting the war on terrorism.[34] This view was at odds with the opinion of John Yoo at OLC and David Addington, legal counsel to Vice President Cheney, who insisted the "unitary executive," (i.e. the president), could not be unduly limited by Congress in exercising his wartime powers as commander in chief.[35] While the 2004 Supreme Court decisions gave the administration the opportunity to go to Congress to put the terrorism program as a whole on a strong statutory foundation, Bush officials declined to do so. It would take a more forceful Supreme Court decision to prompt the administration to seek legislative support.

That decision came in *Hamdan v. Rumsfeld* (2006), wherein the Supreme Court ruled that the administration could not go forward with military commissions without explicit approval from Congress. Furthermore, it held that the basic legal protections of

Common Article 3 of the Geneva Conventions applied as a treaty obligation in the war against the al-Qaeda network. Of even greater concern for the administration, the court's holding implied that the 1996 War Crimes Act was applicable to the administration's treatment of detainees. The decision that the Geneva Conventions and the War Crimes Act applied in the fight against al-Qaeda alarmed the CIA, which feared retroactive discipline to those involved in its interrogation program. In sum, the Supreme Court's decision had struck at the core of the legal basis for the administration's policies regarding detainees, interrogation and military commissions.[36] The New York Times' Linda Greenhouse, among the nation's most respected Supreme Court reporters, called Hamdan v. Rumsfeld (2006) a "sweeping and categorical defeat" for the Bush administration and an "historic event, a defining moment in the ever-shifting balance of power among branches of government...."[37]

To counter this defeat, the Bush administration went to Congress, which backed the president by passing the Military Commissions Act of 2006 (MCA 2006). The act authorized "trial by military commission for violations of the law of war, and for other purposes."[38] It also gave the president a broadened definition of an unlawful enemy combatant, provided implicit approval for aggressive interrogations short of torture, granted immunity from prosecution for those who participated in past interrogations, and eliminated judicial habeas corpus review for Guantanamo detainees.[39]

The elimination of habeas corpus challenges by detainees was an update to provisions contained in the Detainee Treatment Act of 2005, which appeared to sit on both sides of the fence in dealing with the detainee issue. On the one hand, the act held that no person under detention in a DoD facility could be subject to any "treatment or technique of interrogation not authorized by and listed in the United States Army Field Manual on Intelligence Interrogation."[40] This seemed to be an effort to eliminate the harsh interrogation measures that had occurred subsequent to Rumsfeld's December 2002 authorization order for techniques based on the SERE program. Yet the Detainee Treatment Act also legislated that "no court, justice, or judge shall have jurisdiction to hear or consider … an application for a writ of habeas corpus filed by or on behalf of an alien detained by the Department of Defense at Guantanamo Bay,"[41] which critics viewed as another assault on due process.

MCA 2006 would expand on the perceived assault on due process. During his appeal for support of MCA 2006, President Bush for the first time announced the use of the government's coercive interrogation program. He stated that his reasons for doing so were twofold. The first reason was that the government had largely completed the process of questioning key detainees, and to "start the process for bringing them to trial, we must bring them into the open."[42] A second reason was that the Supreme Court's decision in *Hamdan v. Rumsfeld* (2006) had impaired, from the president's perspective, the administration's ability to prosecute terrorists through military commissions and called into question the future of the CIA's program on interrogations. Bush went on to note that in its ruling on military commissions, the Supreme Court determined Common Article 3 of the Geneva Conventions applied to the war with al-Qaeda. In Bush's view, and clearly in the view of his legal advisors, the problem with the provisions of Common Article 3 was that its provisions were "vague and undefined, and each could be interpreted in different ways by American or foreign judges."[43]

According to Bush administration critic and legal scholar Christopher Pyle, the passage of MCA 2006 marked the United States as the first nation in the post-World War II era to "legislatively break with the international community on what constitutes war crimes. It absolved all who ordered, encouraged, carried out, and concealed their commission in the past."[44] As Pyle contended, "George W. Bush was the first American president to pre-pardon himself by persuading Congress to grant blanket amnesty for war crimes committed under his authority."[45]

There were many who felt the administration of President Barack Obama would right the alleged wrongs of the Bush administration in terms of coercive interrogations and detainee treatment, and the initial signs pointed in that direction. During a signing ceremony at the White House two days after taking office, President Obama issued an executive order to close the detention facility at Guantanamo Bay, stating that it was necessary to "restore the standards of due process and the core constitutional values that have made this country great even in the midst of war, even in dealing with terrorism."[46] He signed an additional executive order that day, which ended the Bush administration's CIA program of enhanced interrogation by requiring the Army field manual be used as the governing guide for future terrorism interrogations. Obama stated, "We believe that the Army field manual reflects the best judgment of our military, that we can abide by a rule that says we don't torture, but that we can still effectively obtain the intelligence that we need."[47]

Yet in spite of these executive orders, Guantanamo remains open. Additionally, the Obama administration has not pushed Congress to change the definition of torture in the Military Commissions Act of 2006 so that it agrees with international law. The

Military Commissions Act of 2009, introduced after Obama took office, "still defines torture in terms of major organ failure or major bodily injury, which excludes most acts captured by international law."[48] In addition, although the current U.S. Attorney General's office noted Bybee and Yoo had "exercised poor judgment' in their legal opinions paving the way for harsh interrogation techniques, the Obama administration refused to take further action.[49] This is not surprising given Obama's statement while still president-elect that America needed to "look forward as opposed to looking backwards" in regard to the enhanced interrogation issue.[50] Constitutional lawyer Glenn Greenwald contended that by failing to act against those who had written flawed legal opinions with such far-reaching impact, America chose to evade the obligations of the Convention Against Torture. Greenwald argued that those who wanted the Justice Department to refrain from criminal investigations seldom bother to mention our "obligation under the Convention. There isn't even a pretense … to reconcile what they're advocating with the treaty obligations to which Ronald Reagan bound the U.S. in 1988."[51]

The days do appear to be gone in which the United States stood at the forefront in developing international norms for treatment of detainees, as embodied in the post-World War II Geneva Conventions as well as the UN Convention Against Torture. The recent passage of the National Defense Authorization Act (NDAA) for Fiscal Year 2012 further suggests those days are not likely to return. The act has prompted a broad range of criticism from an unlikely mixture of allies, to include Republican Senator Rand Paul, retired Marine generals Charles Krulak and Joseph Hoar, and the American Civil Liberties Union (ACLU). In calling for a veto of the act, Paul noted that its suspension of "certain rights to due process is especially worrisome, given that we are engaged in a war that appears to have no end. Rights given up now cannot be expected to be returned."[52] Krulak and Hoar echoed that view, contending the provisions of the NDAA "would authorize the military to indefinitely detain without charge people suspected of involvement with terrorism, including United States citizens apprehended on American soil. Due process would be a thing of the past."[53]

Ignoring calls for a veto, President Obama signed the NDAA into law on December 31, 2011, but issued a signing statement expressing reservations with the act's provisions regulating the detention and prosecution of suspected terrorists, and noted his "administration will not authorize the indefinite military detention without trial of American citizens."[54] Yet the ACLU contended that the president's signing statement "only applies to how his administration would use the authorities granted by the NDAA, and would not affect how the law is interpreted by subsequent administrations," and criticized the act for its "sweeping worldwide indefinite detention provision."[55]

The main justification for the measures that have been put into place in the decade since 9/11 has been their effectiveness in deterring future acts of terrorism. As noted, these measures placed limits on due process and used "enhanced interrogation techniques" against detainees. Those who support the use of aggressive interrogation techniques view them as controlled measures which do not rise to the level of torture, and insist the procedures yielded invaluable intelligence in the Global War on Terror. With that as the central justification, coercion's utility warrants an assessment.

The Utility of Coercion

As discussed previously, on September 6, 2006, President George Bush announced for the first time that the government had used coercive techniques when questioning suspected terrorists. In defending the CIA program that he had authorized,

14

Bush contended that enhanced interrogation had saved lives and was vital to U.S. national security, and he shared specific examples of its success. His claims have served as the basis for defending the program in the years since the announcement.

Bush's first example of success was information provided by Abu Zubaydah, mentioned earlier as an independent terrorist facilitator who was the first person subjected to waterboarding by the administration. The president stated Abu Zubaydah was initially uncooperative during questioning but then began to provide invaluable information after being subjected to "alternative procedures" employed by CIA interrogators.[56] According to the president, Abu Zubaydah "disclosed Khalid Sheikh Mohammed – or KSM – was the mastermind behind the 9/11 attacks, and used the alias 'Mukhtar.'"[57] Furthermore, Bush claimed that Abu Zubaydah "identified one of KSM's accomplices in the 9/11 attacks – a terrorist named Ramzi bin al Shibh. The information Zubaydah provided helped lead to the capture of bin al Shibh," who ultimately led investigators to KSM.[58] In Bush's account, the enhanced interrogation of KSM in turn provided significant details of other terrorist plots, to include planned attacks on buildings in the United States. Thus, as the president explained to the American people, vital intelligence was obtained through the CIA's program. Bush did not provide specific methods used during the interrogations, claiming that doing so would help the terrorists learn how to "resist questioning," but he stated the "procedures were tough, and they were safe, and lawful, and necessary."[59]

There are many facts that Bush ignored while crediting the role of enhanced interrogation in combating terrorism, such as the fact that the FBI confirmed al-Qaeda's responsibility for 9/11 shortly after the attacks through the non-coercive interrogation of

15

Abu Jandal, who had been arrested by Yemeni officials after the October 2000 bombing of the USS *Cole*. Still in Yemeni custody at the time of the 9/11 attacks, Abu Jandal identified many of the 9/11 hijackers to FBI and NCIS interrogators and provided "invaluable intelligence on al-Qaeda's structure, operatives and operations," all without being subjected to coercive techniques.[60]

Bush also omitted or distorted key facts when heralding the success in interrogating Abu Zubaydah through enhanced techniques. The president failed to note that after Abu Zubaydah's capture in late March 2002, FBI special agent Ali Soufan conducted the initial interrogation. Soufan was an excellent choice given his demonstrated skills in leading the successful interrogation of Abu Jandal cited above. In testimony before Congress, Soufan acknowledged that Abu Zubaydah was responsive to traditional, non-coercive interrogation methods and provided vital intelligence, including details about Khalid Sheikh Mohammed's role as the mastermind behind 9/11.[61] This contradicts Bush's claim that the enhanced interrogation of Abu Zubaydah revealed KSM's nickname of "Mukhtar" and his link to 9/11. Additional examination of the president's claim further exposes its inaccuracy. The CIA received information regarding the "Mukhtar" nickname in August 2001 but failed to process it, as the 9/11 Commission documented in reporting the CIA "failed to focus on information that Khalid Sheikh Mohammed is a key al-Qaeda lieutenant or connect information identifying KSM as the 'Mukhtar' mentioned in other reports to the analysis...."[62]

In addition, Soufan noted that simply by putting together key dates, the falsehoods become even more obvious regarding the success of enhanced techniques, i.e. waterboarding, in the interrogation of Abu Zubaydah. The intelligence community

16

had established the identity of KSM and his role as the 9/11 mastermind in April 2002 through the FBI's non-coercive interrogation of Abu Zubaydah, yet waterboarding was not introduced through OLC verbal approval until July 2002 and through OLC written approval until August 2002.[63] Thus, Bush ignored the CIA's failures in August 2001 to process information that it already had on KSM, choosing instead to give the agency credit for what had actually been an FBI success occurring prior to the incorporation of the "tough" procedures he heralded.

To further support his narrative, Bush claimed that the CIA's enhanced techniques in dealing with Abu Zubaydah led them to Ramzi bin al Shibh, who in reality was captured through information obtained by an FBI interrogation of another terrorist named Ahmed al-Darbi.[64] Other reports indicate the information leading to al Shibh came from the Emir of Qatar, who intelligence officials wished to protect as a source.[65] Regardless, in no account other than Bush's was the arrest of the terrorist linked to the waterboarding of Abu Zubaydah. In addition, the 9/11 Commission noted that had the CIA properly analyzed information it already had on KSM in August 2001, it could have readily established his connection to Ramzi bin al Shibh.[66] Once again, the president ignored the CIA's failures and chose to give unwarranted credit to the agency in his attempt to extol the success of enhanced interrogation techniques.

While debate remains regarding what measures led Pakistani ISI and CIA agents to capture KSM on March 1, 2003, claims regarding the effectiveness of his subsequent enhanced interrogation do not survive close examination. Bush speechwriter Marc Thiessen echoed the president's contention that coercive techniques led to the discovery of additional KSM-designed plots against the United States. Thiessen claimed the waterboarding of the 9/11 mastermind deterred the "Second Wave," which was an attack intended to fly a hijacked airliner into Los Angeles' Library Tower, the tallest building on the West Coast.[67] This "Second Wave" of attacks against America was supposed to come in 2002, but KSM was not captured until the following year, making it impossible for him to have provided information preventing the attack. Such discrepancies greatly undermine their credibility when they trumpet the success of enhanced interrogation techniques.

Arguably, there have been four major intelligence successes in the Global War on Terror. The first was establishing the link between al-Qaeda and 9/11, which, as noted previously, the FBI accomplished through non-coercive means. The other highly significant successes were the capture of Saddam Hussein, the killing of Abu Musab al-Zarqawi, and the killing of Osama bin Laden. An analysis of each event shows that none happened as a result of enhanced interrogation techniques.

In the first months of the Iraq war, the strategy to find the deposed Saddam Hussein had been to go after "the big name players in the defeated government who were on the loose in the hopes that, if caught, they would reveal Saddam's whereabouts."[68] U.S. Army interrogator Eric Maddox arrived in Iraq in July 2003 and quickly discarded the strategy in favor of a less orthodox one focusing on low-level detainees, to include drivers and bodyguards, as well as walk-ins and sources. The intelligence he gained and incorporated into a carefully structured linked diagram led to Muhammad Ibrahim, the man whom Maddox's detective work determined was running the insurgency for Saddam. Maddox had not resorted to harsh interrogation techniques previously, nor did he with Ibrahim, who ultimately led Army personnel to Saddam's hiding place in Tikrit. Staff Sergeant Maddox stated that he never used torture in the process of locating Saddam, mostly because "he doesn't think it works."[69] It should be noted that the efforts of Maddox were supported by a computer team using a program, the "Mongo Link," which processed more than 60,000 relationships in Saddam's circle.[70] Thus, the former leader of Iraq, a man whose removal from power warranted a war in the view of the Bush administration, was captured not through "enhanced interrogation techniques" but by using traditional means combined with advanced technology.

The capture of Abu Musab al-Zarqawi, the brutal leader of al-Qaeda in Iraq, also became a paramount objective for the Bush administration and U.S. military officials. Matthew Alexander led the team of interrogators whose efforts located al-Zarqawi, culminating in the terrorist's death from a targeted U.S. Air Force strike on June 7, 2006. Alexander later explained that the interrogation team was able to locate al-Zarqawi through several carefully orchestrated sessions involving multiple detainees, one of whom ultimately provided the key piece of intelligence leading to the terrorist. The techniques used were non-coercive and based on "respect, rapport, hope, cunning and deception. The old ones – fear and control – are as obsolete as the buggy whip."[71] Alexander personally conducted several hundred interrogations and supervised hundreds more during his career as an interrogator for the U.S. Air Force, and did so without resorting to brutal techniques. Alexander insisted that the keys to success were found in knowledge and patience, stating that "interrogators who were familiar with the detainees' language and culture, and who exhaustively studied each prisoner's case, used charisma and empathy to patiently elicit vital intelligence."[72]

Alexander's techniques are reflected in those used by Ali Soufan, who was among America's most successful interrogators prior to and following the 9/11 attacks. Soufan employed what he termed the "Informed Interrogation Approach," which is based on "leveraging our knowledge of the detainee's culture and mindset, together with using information we already know about him."[73]

Knowledge and patience rather than force led to perhaps the most significant intelligence success since 9/11, namely the killing of Osama bin Laden. Yet within days of President Obama's announcement that the United States had conducted an operation that killed the terrorist, the unrepentant John Yoo claimed, "President George W. Bush, not his successor, constructed the interrogation and warrantless surveillance programs that produced this week's actionable intelligence."[74] The interrogation program to which Yoo referred was that of enhanced interrogation. Former attorney general Michael Mukasey echoed Yoo's claim, stating intelligence leading to the al-Qaeda leader could be traced to Khalid Sheikh Mohammed, "who broke like a dam under the pressure of harsh interrogation techniques that included waterboarding. He loosed a torrent of information – including eventually the nickname of a trusted courier of bin Laden."[75] Much like the claims made by other advocates for enhanced interrogation, Yoo and Mukasey's statements would turn out to be false.

When President Obama announced bin Laden's death on May 1, 2011, he stated that "last August, after years of painstaking work by our intelligence community, I was briefed on a possible lead to bin Laden."[76] Senator John McCain discussed that lead and the role of intelligence with CIA Director Leon Panetta shortly after the death of bin Laden; based on that discussion, McCain revealed the first mention of "Abu Ahmed al-

Kuwaiti – the nickname of the al-Qaeda courier who ultimately led us to bin Laden ...

came from a detainee held in another country, who we believe was not tortured."[77]

McCain also stated that the use of enhanced interrogation techniques on Khalid Sheikh

Mohammed, who was waterboarded 183 times, produced "false and misleading

information. He specifically told his interrogators that Abu Ahmed had moved to

Peshawar ... and ceased his role as an al-Qaeda facilitator – none of which was true."[78]

None of the three detainees who the CIA acknowledges having waterboarded, i.e. Abu

Zubaydah, KSM and Abdul Rahim al-Nashiri, ever provided Abu Ahmed's real name,

his location or an accurate description of his role. Further supported by evidence from

the staff of the Senate Select Committee on Intelligence (SSCI), McCain acknowledged

that the intelligence ultimately leading to bin Laden was obtained through standard, non-

coercive means.[79]

Just as the advocates of enhanced interrogation techniques give credit where it

is not due, so too do they consistently fail to mention the case of Ibn al-Shaykh al-Libi,

whose false intelligence obtained through harsh procedures had catastrophic

consequences. Al-Libi was an independent terrorist who worked with Abu Zubaydah in

running the Khaldan training camp in Afghanistan. After the capture of al-Libi, FBI

agents interrogated him, and their non-coercive techniques yielded actionable

intelligence that prevented an attack against the U.S. embassy in Yemen.[80] However,

the CIA took al-Libi away from the FBI and rendered him to another country, where he

was tortured. During his brutal interrogation sessions, he "confessed" there were

connections between al-Qaeda and Saddam Hussein. As the SSCI noted in its 2006

report on Iraq's weapons of mass destruction (WMD) programs, the CIA "relied heavily on the information obtained from the debriefing of detainee Ibn al-Shaykh al-Libi … to assess Iraq's potential CBW training of al-Qa'ida."[81] In a January 2003 CIA paper on Iraqi support to terrorism, the agency claimed al-Libi told a foreign intelligence service, "Iraq … agreed to provide unspecified chemical or biological weapons training for two al-Qa'ida associates … in December 2000. The two individuals departed for Iraq but did not return, so al-Libi was not in a position to know if any training had taken place."[82]

In spite of al-Libi's inability to confirm the training had actually taken place, the link between al-Qaeda and Saddam Hussein had been established for an administration that appeared to be desperately seeking one as part of its justification for invading Iraq. Bush spread al-Libi's falsehoods in a speech in Cincinnati on October 7, 2002, claiming his administration had "learned that Iraq has trained al-Qaeda members in bomb-making and poisons and deadly gases"[83] Bush made no mention of the fact that the intelligence creating the link was unsubstantiated and had been obtained through torture. As revealed in the Senate report, al-Libi claimed during his initial debriefings that "he lied to the (foreign government service) about future operations to avoid torture."[84] Al-Libi stated the foreign government service asked him about "al-Qa'ida's connections with Iraq" and proceeded to beat him when he said it was a subject about which he knew nothing; "after the beating," al-Libi provided the interrogators with the bogus information that would eventually make its way into CIA reporting.[85] In spite of Defense Intelligence Agency (DIA) assessments that Iraq was unlikely to have provided bin Laden with any useful chemical/biological knowledge yet likely that al-Libi was "intentionally misleading the debriefers,"[86] Director of Central Intelligence George Tenet included the fabrications in the presentation given by Colin Powell to the United Nations on February 5, 2003. According to Powell's Chief of Staff Lawrence Wilkerson, the secretary of state was so frustrated by the weak intelligence he had received in preparing for his speech that he was "about to throw the whole thing out."[87] Powell changed his mind when Tenet arrived and said the intelligence community had a "high-level al-Qaeda figure who had just told them that al-Qaeda and Saddam Hussein's secret police trained together in Baghdad – and chemical and biological weapons were involved."[88] The "high-level" figure was al-Libi, but when Tenet vouched for the source's credibility to Powell, he failed to mention the DIA's doubts.

In his momentous February 2003 speech to the United Nations Security Council, Powell argued the case for a preemptive strike against Iraq and announced that al-Qaeda "continues to have a deep interest in acquiring weapons of mass destruction."[89] Furthermore, Powell claimed that he could "trace the story of a senior terrorist operative telling how Iraq provided training in these weapons to al-Qaeda."[90] Although not mentioned by name, the "senior terrorist operative" was al-Libi. In his speech, Powell also insisted every statement he was to make that day was "backed up by sources, solid sources. These are not assertions. What we're giving you are facts and conclusions based on solid intelligence."[91] Nearly one year to the day after Powell's testimony, al-Libi recanted the purportedly solid intelligence obtained through harsh interrogation techniques. At the time he recanted, al-Libi was back in CIA custody in Afghanistan after his rendition to Egypt. On February 4 and February 5, 2004, CIA officers in Afghanistan sent cables to headquarters in Langley stating that al-Libi's story of links between Iraq and al-Qaeda could no longer be considered reliable.[92] On July 22, 2004, the 9/11 Commission issued its final report on the terrorist attacks upon the

United States, declaring there was no known "collaborative operational relationship" between Saddam Hussein and al-Qaeda.[93] By then, it was irrelevant; the United States was already at war in Iraq.

The Morality of Coercion

In spite of evidence revealing the unreliable nature of intelligence obtained through harsh techniques, the advocates of enhanced interrogation frequently pose a moral question that warrants discussion. Conservative columnist Charles Krauthammer posed a situation in which he feels that torture becomes a moral imperative. In Krauthammer's scenario, likely derived by confusing the TV series *24* with reality, a terrorist has planted a nuclear bomb in New York City that will go off in one hour, thereby killing millions. Authorities have captured the terrorist, who knows where the bomb is but refuses to reveal its location. The question posed by Krauthammer is whether or not one should be allowed to administer torture in such a case. In his view, "on most issues regarding torture, I confess tentativeness and uncertainty. But on this issue, there can be no uncertainty: Not only is it permissible to hang this miscreant by his thumbs. It is a moral duty."[94] While acknowledging the hypothetical nature of the scenario, Krauthammer defended its relevance by claiming terrorists are often captured with only minutes to spare before the attack they have orchestrated takes place. In his view, "this 'hypothetical' is common enough that the Israelis have a term for precisely that situation: the ticking time bomb problem."[95]

Krauthammer's opinion that one has a moral duty to torture in such a case was shared by law professor Mirko Bagaric, who insisted that "our reflex rejection of torture needs to be replaced by recognition that it can be a moral means of saving lives."[96] Bagaric qualified this by noting torture is only justified in extreme circumstances involving key relevant variables, which consist of (1) a large number of lives at risk, (2) immediate harm, (3) no other means available of obtaining vital information, (4) the detainee is the actual orchestrator of the imminent threat, or (5) is known to possess the information that will halt the threat.[97] In other words, he expressed the ticking time bomb problem.

The initial assertion by Krauthammer that the ticking time bomb problem is commonplace is not supported by evidence issued in a 2004 CIA Inspector General (IG) report titled, "Counterterrorism Detention and Interrogation Activities." In assessing the major threats listed as thwarted by the agency's Counterterrorism Center (CTC) between September 2001 and October 2003, the report stated, "This review did not uncover any evidence that these plots were imminent."[98] The report also recognized that the "effectiveness of particular interrogation techniques (i.e., EIT) in eliciting information that might not otherwise have been obtained cannot be so easily measured, however."[99] Thus, the second and third factors in Bagaric's formulation are discounted by the IG's report. In addition, both the Krauthammer and Bagaric scenarios are based on the highly improbable assumption that the authorities have perfect information in relation to the terrorist's planned activities and knowledge.

Throwing a different moral dimension into the mix, Marc Thiessen, among the most vocal advocates of enhanced interrogation, insisted that it was "never used to gain intelligence. It was used to gain cooperation" and was done so in a controlled manner.[100] By implication, there is nothing immoral about administering allegedly harsh techniques, because their application is done in a controlled manner only designed to achieve compliance. In short, the entire process is relatively benign and by no means immoral. Yet there is "precious little behavioral evidence that torturers have anywhere near the psychological insight or self-control with which they credit themselves."[101] The CIA IG observed that "during the interrogations of two detainees, the waterboard was used in a manner inconsistent with the written DoJ legal opinion of 1 August 2002."[102] The report highlighted that observation with evidence that one key al-Qaeda terrorist (KSM) was "subjected to the waterboard at least 183 times and was denied sleep for a period of 180 hours. In this and another instance, the technique of application and volume of water used differed from the DoJ opinion."[103] Hence, the manner in which waterboarding was applied in reality differed greatly from that envisioned by lawyers generating convoluted legal justifications in a sanitized environment.

The photos from Abu Ghraib and, as of 2006, the deaths of 19 prisoners at the hands of U.S. soldiers and interrogators provided further evidence that application of harsh techniques eventually led to abuse, and further undermined the contention that a controlled environment can be maintained while applying enhanced procedures.[104] Thus, buying into the distinction between "good, rational, utilitarian torture and bad, sadistic torture" is what makes it possible to be persuaded by the indictment that a 'few bad apples'at Abu Ghraib undermined what would have otherwise been an effective program and keeps "alive the fiction of a controlled form of painful torture practiced by more upright torturers."[105]

Taken in full, justifying torture as moral in exceptional circumstances or because it can be administered in a controlled manner emerges as little more than a smokescreen to deflect criticism from something that international treaties and domestic law rejected long ago. In 1988, President Ronald Reagan signed the Convention

Against Torture, which unequivocally states that "no exceptional circumstances whatsoever, whether a state of war or a threat of war, internal political instability or any other public emergency, may be invoked as a justification of torture."[106] In signing the document, Reagan demonstrated the recognition that other nations expect America to serve as a world leader not just politically, economically or militarily, but also in terms of morality. Such morality long defined America as a nation, and justifications for torture on moral grounds succeed only in eroding an essential part of America's foundation.

Conclusion

Prior to 9/11, the United States stood as one of the international community's leading voices against torture. However, the days of Ronald Reagan speaking of torture as an "abhorrent practice"[107] vanished after the terrorist attacks on September 11, 2001, replaced by an environment where lawyers such as Bybee and Yoo labored to justify treating prisoners inhumanely and cast aside international treaties concluding otherwise. According to the strained OLC definitions found in the memos of August 1, 2002, the Bush administration would not be guilty of torture because none of the techniques to be employed in interrogations rose to that level. Yet to determine as the memos did that waterboarding was simply "a controlled, acute episode, lacking the connotation of a protracted period of time generally given to suffering,"[108] requires what Cole referred to as "an affirmative suspension of disbelief."[109]

The OLC memos of August 1, 2002, sought further justification of enhanced interrogation techniques, and waterboarding specifically, by noting that no SERE students subjected to the technique ever displayed "any significant long-term mental health consequences" or "physical harm" as a result.[110] To equate an interrogation administered by one's allies in a training environment with one given by an adversary in

27

wartime is a sophomoric line of reasoning at best. Significantly and unsurprisingly, the CIA's IG considered a comparison of the two to be meaningless, noting "the SERE waterboard experience is so different from the subsequent Agency usage as to make it almost irrelevant."[111]

Yet such irrelevance appeared to make little difference to the OLC lawyers and the members of the Bush administration, just as they ignored evidence that enhanced interrogation techniques were ineffective. As Darius Rejali noted in his comprehensive study of torture, "apologists often assume that torture works, and all that is left is the moral justification. If torture does not work, then their apology is irrelevant."[112] Rejali devoted hundreds of pages and years of research in demonstrating that torture is an ineffective and unreliable means of obtaining information. His opinion was shared by Lieutenant General John Kimmons, former U.S. Army Deputy Chief of Staff for Intelligence. At a September 2006 DoD news briefing in which he discussed the release of the Army's updated field manual for conducting interrogations, Kimmons stated "no good intelligence is going to come from abusive practices. I think history tells us that. I think the empirical evidence of the last five years, hard years, tells us that."[113]

Empirical evidence that might have settled the debate over harsh interrogation techniques existed in the form of CIA videos showing detainees, to include Abu Zubaydah and Abdul Rahim al-Nashiri, being subjected to interrogation. In the cases of Abu Zubaydah and al-Nashiri, the videos showed the waterboarding sessions the two terrorists experienced. Remarkably, Jose Rodriguez, who ran the CIA's CTC from 2002 to 2005, had the videos destroyed in disregard of a court order that they be turned over.[114] John Gannon, a former CIA deputy director, stated that if the tapes had survived to be seen by the public, the debate over enhanced interrogation techniques would have ended, recognizing that to a "spectator, it would look like torture…. And torture is wrong."[115]

The empirical evidence that does exist revealed extremely valuable intelligence came from non-coercive techniques employed in numerous vital cases, to include identifying the perpetrators of the 9/11 attacks, apprehending Saddam Hussein, locating and killing al-Zarqawi, and finding and killing Osama bin Laden. However, the alleged value of notable intelligence successes obtained through harsh interrogation methods did not withstand close scrutiny. In the worst case, that of al-Libi, torture led to false information that became a factor in the Bush administration's decision to go to war in Iraq; such a colossal failure hardly constitutes an endorsement of enhanced interrogation techniques. The empirical evidence also demonstrated that organized coercion yielded poor information by sweeping up ignorant and innocent individuals who overwhelmed investigators with misleading information. As Ali Soufan summarized in testimony before the Senate, it was a mistake to abandon effective and reliable interrogation approaches "in favor of harsh interrogation methods that are harmful, shameful, slower, unreliable, ineffective, and play directly into the enemy's handbook."[116]

Yet playing into the enemy's handbook was precisely what happened through the use of enhanced interrogation techniques that were not just questionable from a legal perspective, but were ill-considered from a policy perspective as well. As a result, in 2008 the United States found itself placed on a torture watch list by staunch ally Canada;[117] it took pressure from U.S. Secretary of State Condoleezza Rice to have

America's name removed. In 2009, a Spanish judge considered charges against six Bush administration officials, including Gonzales, Yoo, Bybee and Addington, for violations of the Convention Against Torture.[118] Again, State Department pressure put a halt to further action, but the inconsistency of America's professed policy in relation to its actions since 9/11 had become clear. As noted in the 2004 CIA IG report previously cited, the "EITs used by the Agency under the CTC program are inconsistent with the public policy positions that the United States has taken regarding human rights."[119] The Senate Armed Services Committee's inquiry into detainee treatment noted such inconsistencies have an impact, as illustrated by a 2007 international BBC poll showing only 29 percent of people around the world said the United States was a "generally positive influence in the world."[120] The fact that America had come to be seen in a negative light by so many "complicates our ability to attract allies to our side, strengthens the hand of our enemies, and reduces our ability to collect intelligence that can save lives."[121] In sum from a policy perspective, the United States sacrificed critical strategic advantage for questionable tactical gain.

Many argue that the total disregard for human life shown by our adversaries justified harsh treatment in return, but supporters of such a view should consider the words of General David Petraeus, who wrote, "Our values and the laws governing warfare teach us to respect human dignity, maintain our integrity, and do what is right. Adherence to our values distinguishes us from our enemy."[122] Petraeus further stated, "This fight depends on securing the population, which must understand that we – not our enemies – occupy the moral high ground.[123]

Philip Zelikow, who served as Executive Director of the 9/11 Commission, believes America's abandonment of its legal and ethical traditions following the terrorist attacks of September 11, 2001, will be viewed years hence in the same way as President Franklin D. Roosevelt's internment of Japanese-Americans during World War II. Both happened, Zelikow believed, because "fear and anxiety were exploited by zealots and fools."[124] We occupied the moral high ground in the past, and we can occupy it again, but not until the fear that 9/11 engendered and the enhanced interrogation techniques that emerged are put to rest.

Endnotes

[1] Frederick A.O. Schwarz Jr. and Aziz Z. Huq, *Unchecked and Unbalanced: Presidential Power in a Time of Terror* (New York: The New Press, 2007), 71.

[2] Dick Cheney with Liz Cheney, *In My Time: A Personal and Political Memoir* (New York: Simon & Schuster, Inc., 2011), 363.

[3] Ibid.

[4] Ibid.

[5] Barack Obama, *National Security Strategy* (Washington, DC: The White House, May 2010), 36.

[6] George W. Bush, *Decision Points* (New York: Crown Publishers, 2010), 155.

[7] White House Counsel Alberto R. Gonzales, "Decisions Re Application of the Geneva Convention on Prisoners of War to the Conflict with Al Qaeda and the Taliban," memorandum for the President of the United States, Washington, DC, January 25, 2001, http://www.hereinreality.com/alberto_gonzales_torture_memo.html (accessed January 3, 2012).

[8] Ibid.

[9] U.S. President George W. Bush, "Humane Treatment of Taliban and al Qaeda Detainees," memorandum for the Vice President, the Secretary of State, the Secretary of Defense, the Attorney General, et. al., Washington, DC, February 7, 2002, http:////www.pegc.us/archive/White_House/bush_memo_20020207_ed.pdf (accessed January 3, 2012).

[10] *The United States Department of Justice, Office of Legal Counsel Home Page*, http://www.justice.gov/olc/ (accessed January 3, 2012).

[11] Jack Goldsmith, *The Terror Presidency: Law and Judgment Inside the Bush Administration* (New York: W.W. Norton & Company, 2007), 33.

[12] U.S. Department of State Bulletin, U.S. Signs UN Convention Against Torture," August 1988, http://findarticles.com/p/articles/mi_m1079/is_n2137_v88/ai_6742034/ (accessed January 1, 2012). The UN Convention Against Torture and Other Cruel, Inhuman or Degrading Treatment or Punishment defines torture as "any act by which severe pain or suffering, whether physical or mental, is intentionally inflicted on a person for such purposes as obtaining from him or a third person information or a confession...." The United States was a key architect in the development of the Convention Against Torture, which was opened for signature at UN Headquarters in New York on February 4, 1985. It was adopted by the UN General Assembly in December 1984 and entered into force in June 1987 after ratification by 20 nations. On April 18, 1988, during the administration of President Ronald Reagan, America became the sixty-third nation to sign the CAT. Reagan stated that the convention marked a "significant step in the development during this century of international measures against torture and other inhuman treatment or punishment." The U.S. Senate ratified the CAT in 1994.

[13] Ali H. Soufan with Daniel Freedman, *The Black Banners: The Inside Story of 9/11 and the War Against al-Qaeda* (New York: W.W. Norton & Company, 2011), 375.

[14] David Cole, ed., *The Torture Memos: Rationalizing the Unthinkable* (New York: The New York Press, 2009), 19.

[15] Ibid.

[16] Assistant Attorney General Jay S. Bybee, "Re: Standards of Conduct for Interrogation under 18 U.S.C. Sections 2340-2340A," memorandum for Alberto R. Gonzales, Counsel to the President, Washington, DC, August 1, 2002, quoted in Cole, *The Torture Memos*, 41.

[17] Jane Mayer, *The Dark Side: The Inside Story of How the War on Terror Turned into a War on American Ideals* (New York: Doubleday Publishing Group, 2008), 171.

[18] Goldsmith, *The Terror Presidency*, 148.

[19] Ibid, 149. The War Crimes Act of 1996 was another noteworthy law emphasizing American opposition to torture prior to 9/11. The law's sponsor was a conservative member of Congress from North Carolina who proposed it after meeting a survivor of North Vietnam's notorious "Hanoi Hilton." Congressional support for the War Crimes Act was overwhelming, as illustrated by its unanimous passage in the Senate and the passage in the House by the noncontroversial measure of voice vote. The legislation imposed criminal penalties in the United States for "grave breaches" – which included torture – of the Geneva Conventions. See R. Jeffrey Smith, "Detainee Abuse Charges Feared," *Washington Post*, July 28, 2006.

[20] Cole, *The Torture Memos*, 20.

[21] Goldsmith, *The Terror Presidency*, 144.

[22] Ibid, 151.

[23] Brian Ross and Richard Esposito, "CIA Harsh Interrogation Techniques Described," November 18, 2005, http://abcnews.go.com/Blotter/Investigation/story?id=1322866 (accessed January 7, 2012).

[24] U.S. Congress, Senate, Committee on Armed Services, *Inquiry into the Treatment of Detainees in U.S. Custody*, 110th Cong., 2nd sess., November 20, 2008, xiii.

[25] Ibid.

[26] Ibid, xvii.

[27] Ibid, xix.

[28] Ibid, xxi.

[29] George R. Fay, Investigating Officer, *AR 15-6 Investigation of the Abu Ghraib Detention Facility and 205th Military Intelligence Brigade* (Unclassified), 8.

[30] Goldsmith, *The Terror Presidency*, 108. The most dangerous "high-value" detainees were kept at secret locations elsewhere. These secret CIA prisons, as well as the associated extraordinary rendition, would generate controversy when news of their use surfaced in late 2005.

[31] Christopher H. Pyle, *Getting Away with Torture: Secret Government, War Crimes, and the Rule of Law* (Washington, DC: Potomac Books, Inc., 2009), 81.

[32] Linda Greenhouse, "The Supreme Court: Detainees; Access to Courts," June 29, 2004. http://www.nytimes.com/2004/06/29/us/the-supreme-court-detainees-access-to-courts.html (accessed January 5, 2012). Full text of *Hamdi v. Rumsfeld*, June 28, 2004, found at http://www.law.cornell.edu/supct/html/03-6696.ZO.html (accessed January 5, 2012).

[33] Steven C. Welsh, "*Rasul v. Bush* Supreme Court Guantanamo Decision: Summary and Analysis," June 30, 2004, http://www.cdi.org/friendlyversion/printversion.cfm?documentID=3456 (accessed January 5, 2012).

[34] U.S. Supreme Court, *Hamdi v. Rumsfeld*, June 28, 2004.

[35] Goldsmith, *The Terror Presidency*, 85.

[36] Ibid, 137.

[37] Linda Greenhouse, "Justices, 5-3, Broadly Reject Bush Plan to Try Detainees," *New York Times*, June 30, 2006.

[38] Public Law 109-366-Oct. 17, 2006, "Military Commissions Act of 2006," pdf file.

[39] Goldsmith, *The Terror Presidency*, 139.

[40] "Detainee Treatment Act of 2005," December 30, 2005, http://cjc.delaware.gov/PDF/The%20Detainee%20Treatment%20Act%20of%202005.pdf (accessed January 7, 2012).

[41] Ibid.

[42] George W. Bush, "President Discusses Creation of Military Commissions to Try Suspected Terrorists," September 6, 2006 http://georgewbush-whitehouse.archives.gov/news/releases/2006/09/20060906-3.html (accessed January 5, 2012).

[43] Ibid.

[44] Pyle, *Getting Away with Torture*, 167.

[45] Ibid.

[46] "Obama Signs Order to Close Guantanamo Bay Facility," January 22, 2009, CNN web site, http://edition.cnn.com/2009/POLITICS/01/22/guantanamo.order/index.html (accessed January 7, 2012).

[47] Ibid. The previous Army Field Manual governing interrogation was FM 35-42, *Intelligence Interrogation*, dated 28 September 1992. It has been superseded by FM 2-22.3, *Human Intelligence Collector Operations*, dated 6 September 2006.

[48] Darius Rejali, "Torture and Democracy: What Now?" from *Torture: Power, Democracy, and the Human Body*, Shampa Biswas and Zahi Zalloua, eds. (Seattle: University of Washington Press, 2011), 39.

[49] Carrie Johnson and Julie Tate, "Authors of Waterboarding Memos won't be Disciplined," February 20, 2010, http://www.washingtonpost.com/wp-dyn/content/article/2010/02/19/AR2010021904157.html (accessed January 8, 2012). Of note, the Justice Department's Office of Professional Responsibility issued a report in July 2009 that concluded John Yoo and Jay Bybee were guilty of professional misconduct. However, both were spared disbarment when David Margolis, the lone arbiter in reviewing the OPR report, determined the opinions of Yoo and Bybee contained significant flaws but not at the level of intentional professional misconduct.

[50] Mark Memmott, "Obama: Time to Look Forward, but Bush Aides aren't Above the Law," January 11, 2009, http://content.usatoday.com/communities/theoval/post/2009/01/61177294/1 (accessed January 8, 2012).

[51] Glenn Greenwald, "Do We Still Pretend That We Abide By Treaties?" February 16, 2009, http://www.salon.com/opinion/greenwald/2009/02/16/treaties/index.html (accessed January 9, 2012).

[52] Rand Paul, "War On Terror Doesn't Justify Retreat on Rights," *Washington Times*, December 1, 2011.

[53] Charles C. Krulak and Joseph P. Hoar, "Guantanamo Forever?" December 12, 2011, http://www.nytimes.com/2011/12/13/opinion/guantanamo-forever.html (accessed January 8, 2012).

[54] Barack Obama, "Signing Statement to NDAA for FY 12," December 31, 2011 http://proudprogressive.newsvine.com/commander-in-chief (accessed January 8, 2012).

[55] American Civil Liberties Union, "President Obama Signs Indefinite Detention Bill into Law," December 31, 2011, http://www.aclu.org/national-security/president-obama-signs-indefinite-detention-bill-law (accessed January 8, 2012).

[56] Bush, "President Discusses Creation of Military Commissions to Try Suspected Terrorists."

[57] Ibid.

[58] Ibid.

[59] Ibid.

[60] Ali H. Soufan with Daniel Freedman, *The Black Banners: The Inside Story of 9/11 and the War Against al-Qaeda* (New York: W.W. Norton & Company, 2011), 547.

[61] Ali H. Soufan, "Testimony to the Senate Committee on the Judiciary," May 13, 2009, http://www.judiciary.senate.gov/hearings/testimony.cfm?id=e655f9e2809e5476862f735da14945 e6&wit_id=e655f9e2809e5476862f735da14945e6-1-2 (accessed January 1, 2012).

[62] 9/11 Commission, *The 9/11 Commission Report: Final Report of the National Commission on Terrorist Attacks Upon the United States* (New York: W.W. Norton & Company, 2004), 356.

[63] Soufan, "Testimony to the Senate Committee on the Judiciary."

[64] Soufan, *The Black Banners*, 553.

[65] Mayer, *The Dark Side*, 175.

[66] 9/11 Commission, *The 9/11 Commission Report*, 356.

[67] Marc Thiessen, "Enhanced Interrogations Worked," April 21, 2009, http://www.washingtonpost.com/wp-dyn/content/article/2009/04/20/AR2009042002818.html

[68] "U.S. Intelligence Officer Reveals Secret Story of Saddam Hussein's Capture," December 12, 2008, *Fox News* web site http://www.foxnews.com/story/0,2933,466028,00.html# (accessed January 12, 2012).

[69] Ibid. For a detailed account of the capture of Saddam Hussein, see Eric Maddox with Davin Seay, *Mission: Black List #1* (New York: HarperCollins Publishers, 2008).

[70] Darius Rejali, *Torture and Democracy* (Princeton, New Jersey: Princeton University Press, 2007), 509.

[71] Matthew Alexander with John R. Bruning, *How to Break a Terrorist: The U.S. Interrogators Who Used Brains, Not Brutality, to Take Down the Deadliest Man in Iraq,* (New York: Free Press, 2008), 6.

[72] Steven Kleinman and Matthew Alexander, "Try a Little Tenderness," *New York Times*, March 10, 2009.

[73] Soufan, "Testimony to the Senate Committee on the Judiciary."

[74] John Yoo, "From Guantanamo to Abbottabad," May 4, 2011, http://online.wsj.com/article/SB10001424052748703834804576301032595527372.html?mod=WSJ_Opinion_LEADTop (accessed January 12, 2012).

[75] John McCain, "Bin Laden's death and the debate over torture," *Washington Post*, May 11, 2011.

[76] Barack Obama, "Remarks by the President on Osama bin Laden," http://www.whitehouse.gov/the-press-office/2011/05/02/remarks-president-osama-bin-laden (accessed January 12, 2012).

[77] McCain, "Bin Laden's death and the debate over torture."

[78] Ibid.

[79] Ibid.

[80] Soufan, *The Black Banners*, 450.

[81] U.S. Congress, Senate, Select Committee on Intelligence, *Postwar Findings About Iraq's WMD Programs and Links to Terrorism and How They Compare With Prewar Assessments*, 109th Cong., 2nd sess., September 8, 2006, 76.

[82] Ibid.

[83] George W. Bush, "President Bush Outlines Iraqi Threat," October 7, 2002, http://georgewbush-whitehouse.archives.gov/news/releases/2002/10/20021007-8.html (accessed January 12, 2012)

[84] U.S. Congress, *Postwar Findings About Iraq's WMD Programs and Links to Terrorism and How They Compare With Prewar Assessments*, 80.

[85] Ibid, 81

[86] Ibid, 77.

[87] Mayer, *The Dark Side*, 137.

[88] Ibid.

[89] Colin Powell, "U.S. Secretary of State's Address to the United Nations Security Council," February 5, 2003, http://www.guardian.co.uk/world/2003/feb/05/iraq.usa (accessed January 12, 2012).

[90] Ibid.

[91] Ibid.

[92] Mayer, *The Dark* Side, 138.

[93] 9/11 Commission, *The 9/11 Commission Report*, 66.

[94] Charles Krauthammer, "The Truth about Torture," December 5, 2005, http://www.weeklystandard.com/Content/Public/Articles/000/000/006/400rhqav.asp (accessed January 14, 2012).

[95] Ibid.

[96] Mirko Bagaric and Julie Clarke, *Torture: When the Unthinkable is Morally Permissible* (Albany, New York: State University of New York Press, 2007), vii.

[97] Ibid, 34.

[98] Central Intelligence Agency Inspector General, "Special Review: Counterterrorism Detention and Interrogation Activities" (September 2001-October 2003) (2003-7123-IG), 7 May 2004, 88.

[99] Ibid, 100.

[100] Elisabeth Rosen, "Former Bush speechwriter defends 'enhanced interrogation techniques,'" October 28, 2011, http://www.news.cornell.edu/stories/Oct11/ SpeechwriterCover.html (accessed January 18, 2012).

[101] Rejali, *Torture and Democracy*, 453.

[102] CIA IG, "Special Review: Counterterrorism Detention and Interrogation Activities," 103.

[103] Ibid, 104.

[104] Lauren Wilcox, "Dying is Not Permitted," in *Torture: Power, Democracy and the Human Body,* eds. Shampa Biswas and Zahi Zalloua (Seattle: University of Washington Press, 2011), 114.

[105] Ibid, 8.

[106] *UN Convention Against Torture*, part 1, art. 2, sec. 2.

[107] *U.S. Department of State Bulletin*, "U.S. Signs UN Convention Against Torture."

[108] Bybee, quoted in Cole, *The Torture Memos*, 118.

[109] Cole, *The Torture Memos*, 9.

[110] Bybee, quoted in Cole, *The Torture Memos*, 112.

[111] Central Intelligence Inspector General, "Special Review: Counterterrorism Detention and Interrogation Activities," quoted in Cole, *The Torture Memos*, 191.

[112] Rejali, *Torture and Democracy*, 447.

[113] John Kimmons, "DoD News Briefing with Deputy Assistant Secretary Stimson and Lt. Gen. Kimmons from the Pentagon," (The Pentagon: Office of the Assistant Secretary of Defense for Public Affairs, September 6, 2006).

[114] Massimo Calabresi, "Ex-CIA Counterterror Chief: 'Enhanced Interrogation' Led U.S. to bin Laden," May 4, 2011, http://swampland.time.com/2011/05/04/did-torture-get-the-us-osama-bin-laden/ (accessed December 26, 2011).

[115] Mayer, *The Dark Side*, 321.

[116] Soufan, "Testimony to the Senate Committee on the Judiciary."

[117] David Ljunggren, "Canada places U.S., Israel on torture watch list," *Reuters*, January 19, 2008.

[118] Marlise Simons, "Spanish Court Weighs Inquiry on Torture for 6 Bush-Era Officials," March 28, 2009, http://www.nytimes.com/2009/03/29/world/europe/29spain.html (accessed January 14, 2012).

[119] CIA IG, "Special Review: Counterterrorism Detention and Interrogation Activities," 91.

[120] U.S. Congress, *Inquiry into the Treatment of Detainees in U.S. Custody*, xxv.

[121] Ibid.

[122] David Petraeus, "Letter to the troops from the Commanding General," May 10, 2007, http://www.globalsecurity.org/military/library/policy/army/other/petraeus_values-msg_torture070510.htm (accessed January 16, 2012).

[123] Ibid.

[124] Mayer, *The Dark Side*, 335.